Snap, Crackle

BY KATHY FRENCH

Table of Contents

It's Electric

Think about all the things you did today. Did you switch on a light, watch television, or play a battery-run video game? Did you toast bread, listen to the radio, or talk on the telephone? If so, you know the important role electricity plays in your daily life. Electricity makes life easier, more comfortable, and more fun.

▲ A carnival wouldn't be a carnival without electricity. The sights, sounds, and rides of a carnival depend on electricity to work.

You are probably familiar with lightning. But did you know that lightning is a powerful form of electricity that occurs in nature? The electricity in a lightning bolt can be a million times more powerful than the electricity from an outlet in your home.

In this book you will find out what electricity is, how it is produced, and how people can use it safely.

▲ Lightning is a beautiful but dangerous form of electricity.

For thousands of years, people have been curious about electricity and have tried to understand what it is. The ancient Greeks made progress when they discovered an unusual property of hardened tree sap, or amber.

The Greeks noticed that amber, or *elektron* as they called it, attracted little pieces of dust and straw after being rubbed with a piece of fur. The Greeks did not really understand what was happening. But the first observations of electricity had been made. In fact, the word "electricity" comes from the Greek word *elektron*.

Amber like this was used by the Greeks in their experiments with electricity.
▼

Benjamin Franklin conducted experiments ▶
with lightning and invented the first
lightning rod.

In the mid-1700s, Benjamin Franklin performed experiments that proved lightning was a form of electricity. Franklin flew a kite in a thunderstorm. He studied the lightning as it hit the kite and traveled to earth through the kite's string. The strength of the lightning was so great that Franklin was knocked out two times!

Using what he learned, Franklin invented the lightning rod. It was a pointed metal pole. The pointed end was placed above the roof of a building. The other end was planted in the ground. The rod would attract lightning and direct it to the ground. That way the lightning would not harm the building.

◀ Tall buildings are protected
from lightning by lightning
rods. A lightning rod provides
a safe path for lightning
directly into the ground.

5

In the late 1800s, Thomas Edison invented ways to bring electricity into people's homes. Before that time, people had to use candles, oil lamps, or fireplaces to light their homes. Edison designed machines called generators that produced large amounts of electricity. Edison also designed better electric light bulbs that would last longer and give off more light.

Thomas Edison is shown in his laboratory in Menlo Park, New Jersey, with one of the light bulbs he invented. ▼

Today, many of the devices people use at home and work are run by electricity. Washing machines, refrigerators, ovens, vacuum cleaners, elevators, and computers all need electricity to operate. Can you imagine how difficult it would be to do some of your chores without electricity to run the various appliances?

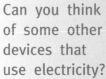

Can you think of some other devices that use electricity?

Static Electricity

Have you ever walked across a rug, reached for the doorknob, and gotten zapped by an electric shock? Or have you ever taken your clothes from the clothes dryer and noticed that some of them stick together? These things happen because of **static electricity**.

To understand static electricity, you must know about the small particles that make up all things. These tiny particles are called **atoms**. Atoms are made of even smaller particles. Three of the most important particles are called protons, neutrons, and electrons. Protons and neutrons are found in the **nucleus** (NOO-klee-uhs), or center, of the atom. Electrons move around the nucleus.

neon atom

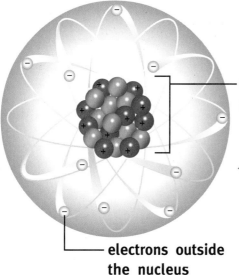

nucleus containing protons and neutrons

◄ Protons and neutrons are found in the nucleus of an atom. Electrons move around the nucleus.

electrons outside the nucleus

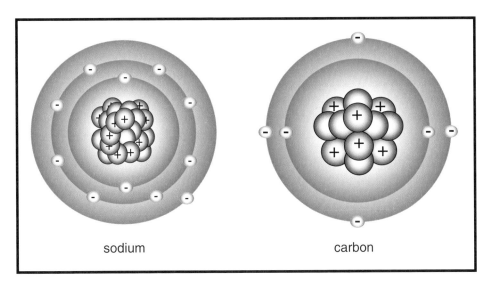

sodium   carbon

▲ These are atoms of sodium and carbon. Notice that the number
of protons (positive charge) equals the number of electrons
(negative charge) in each atom.

The particles that make up an atom differ from
one another. One difference is called **charge**. Charge
is a property that cannot be seen. But its effects—
especially how it makes particles behave—can be
observed.

A **proton** has a positive charge (+). An **electron**
has a negative charge (−). A **neutron** has no charge.

A positive charge and a negative charge cancel
each other out. Because an atom usually has equal
numbers of protons (+) and electrons (−), it is
neutral. It has no overall charge.

If you rub two objects together, electrons can move from one object to the other. This means that one object gains electrons and the other object loses electrons. The object that gains electrons will have a negative charge. The object that loses electrons will have a positive charge.

When electrons are transferred from one object to another without any further movement, it is called static electricity. If you walk across a carpet, electrons move from the carpet to you. You now have extra electrons. When you touch a doorknob, the electrons move from you to the doorknob. This movement of charge is called a discharge. A discharge can be felt as a small shock or seen as a spark. Sometimes a crackling noise can be heard.

◄ A discharge of static electricity can be seen as a spark.

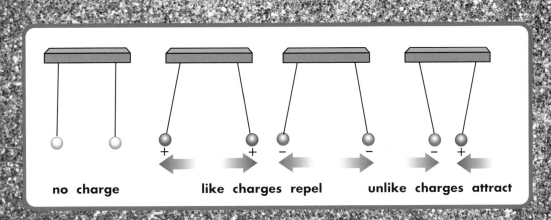

no charge   like charges repel   unlike charges attract

Like charges repel each other. Opposite charges attract each other.

If two objects have different charges, they will attract each other. This means they will pull toward each other. If two objects have the same charge, they will repel each other. This means they will push away from each other. A simple way to remember this is: unlike charges attract; like charges repel.

When your clothes are in a clothes dryer, they rub against one another. Some of the clothes lose their electrons and have a positive charge. Other clothes gain those electrons and have a negative charge. The negatively charged clothes will attract the positively charged clothes, causing them to stick together.

Lightning is a large, dramatic discharge of static electricity. It is no different from the shock you get when you touch a doorknob. It's just bigger!

During a storm, droplets of water and ice in clouds rub against one another. Electrons move from one droplet to another. Positively charged droplets and negatively charged droplets build up in different parts of the clouds. When many electrons build up, they may move quickly to earth, to another cloud, or within the cloud in a huge spark. We call this spark a bolt of lightning.

As electrons jump through the air, they produce intense heat. The heat causes the air to expand suddenly and rapidly. This expansion is the thunder you hear.

▲
Lightning can form between a cloud and the ground, between clouds, or between different parts of one cloud. Which kind is shown in the photo?

Static electricity can cause objects to attract or repel each other. What will happen when you remove electrons from your hair with a comb and bring the comb toward a small stream of water?

WHAT YOU NEED
- hard plastic comb
- water faucet

WHAT TO DO

1. Turn the water faucet on so that the water runs out in a small stream about $\frac{1}{8}$ inch (0.3 centimeter) thick.
2. Bring the comb near the stream of water from the faucet. Observe what happens.
3. Comb your dry hair several times with the comb.
4. Slowly bring the comb near the stream of water from the faucet. Observe what happens.
5. Describe what happens to the stream of water in steps 2 and 4. Why does it happen?

Electricity on the Move

A vacuum cleaner is a device that uses electricity to do work. Have you ever looked at the cord that connects the vacuum cleaner to the wall outlet? It is covered with plastic and the prongs that fit into the socket are metal. Both plastic and metal are used to make electrical cords because of the way they allow electricity to go through them.

Plastic does not allow electricity to go through it easily. Materials that do not allow electricity to flow through them easily are called **insulators**. Other insulators are rubber, glass, wood, and air.

Plastic and rubber are insulators of electricity. Metals are conductors of electricity.
▼

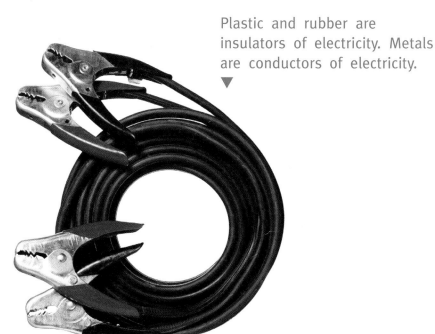

A **conductor** allows electricity to travel through it easily. Most metals—such as copper, gold, and silver—are good conductors of electricity. That is why the wires inside the electrical cords on appliances are made of copper.

Water is also a good conductor of electricity. You should never use electrical devices around water. You could receive a shock if the electricity from the device traveled through the water to you. You could also receive a shock if the electricity traveled from the device through you and then through the water to the earth. The earth is also a good conductor.

"UNPLUG IT"
DO NOT REMOVE THIS TAG!
WARN CHILDREN OF THE RISK OF DEATH
BY ELECTRIC SHOCK!

UT-1

DRYER STOPPED?
Disturbances in your electrical current can trigger the Safety Plug. Press the RESET button until it clicks. Your dryer will resume operation.

This label warns you not to use this device near water. ▲

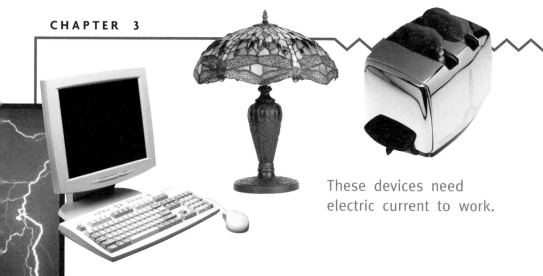

These devices need electric current to work.

The electricity that you use when you plug a vacuum cleaner into a wall outlet is not static electricity. For an electrical device to be useful, electrons have to keep moving through the device. A steady flow of electrons is called an **electric current.** A toaster, lamp, and computer are just a few devices that run on an electric current.

It's a Fact!

A battery contains chemicals that react to make an electric current. Batteries are used to power small electrical devices such as watches, flashlights, and hand-held video games. Batteries are also used in cars. Some batteries stop working when their chemicals no longer react. Others can be recharged and used many times.

Have you ever seen athletes running on a track? The track is a path that the runners must stay on. It is a closed path. It has no breaks or gaps in it. Electric current also needs a path to flow through in order to do work. The path that an electric current flows through is called a circuit.

When a circuit is closed, the electrons have a complete path to travel through. There are no breaks or gaps in the path. When you turn a light switch to the "on" position, you are making a closed circuit.

Closed Circuit

light bulb

direction of electron flow

wire

switch

source of electricity

− +

▲ This is an example of a closed circuit. You can tell that the path for the electric current is complete because the bulb lights up.

Point

TALK ABOUT IT

With a group member, compare and contrast a closed circuit and an open circuit.

When a circuit is open, the path of the electrons is incomplete. There are breaks or gaps in the path. No electrons will flow through an open circuit. When you turn a light switch to the "off" position, you are opening the circuit. This stops the flow of electrons and the light goes out. Many electrical devices turn on and off when you close or open their circuits.

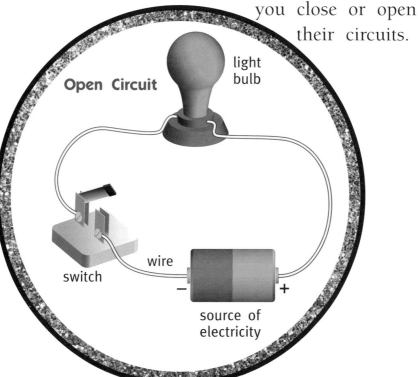

Open Circuit

light bulb

wire

switch

source of electricity

− +

▲ This is an example of an open circuit. You can tell that the path for the electric current is incomplete because the bulb does not light up.

An electrical circuit must have at least three parts: a power source, wires that carry the electricity from the power source, and an object that uses the electricity. A circuit may also contain a switch to open and close it. When you turn on your television set, electricity flows from the wall outlet through the cord and into your television.

This bank of television sets can operate only when there is a closed circuit.

▼

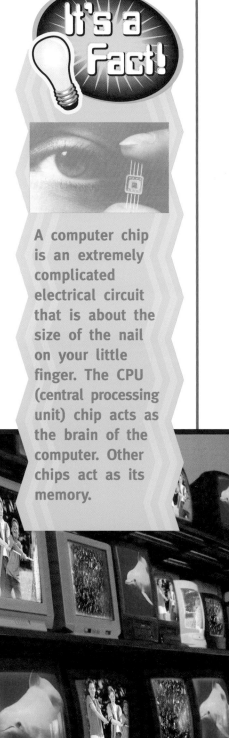

It's a Fact!

A computer chip is an extremely complicated electrical circuit that is about the size of the nail on your little finger. The CPU (central processing unit) chip acts as the brain of the computer. Other chips act as its memory.

19

Kinds of Circuits

Take a minute to look around you and count the number of objects in the room that use electricity. There are quite a few, aren't there? All the objects you counted are parts of a large circuit that may include several rooms in your school or home. There are two ways in which a closed circuit can be set up—in series or in parallel.

▼ What other electrical devices can you find in this picture?

light

dishwasher

microwave oven

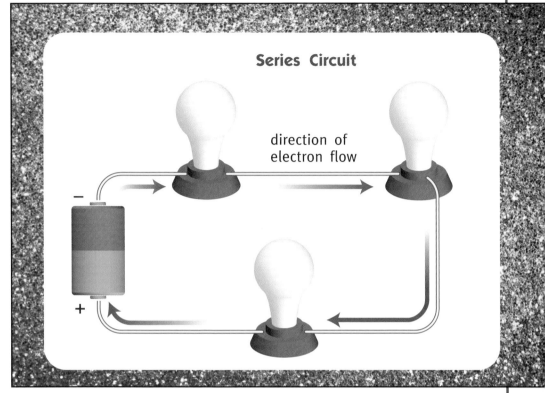

Series Circuit

direction of electron flow

▲ In a series circuit, either all of the parts work or none of them work.

In a **series circuit**, all parts of the circuit are connected in one big loop. The electric current going through a series circuit can follow only one path. If any part of the series circuit is broken or removed, an open circuit is created. None of the other parts of the circuit will work.

If the devices in your home were wired in a series circuit, this could be a problem. If you were watching television in a room with a light on and someone turned the light off, the television would go off, too!

▲
Many household alarm systems are based on a series circuit.

A series circuit is useful in a simple security alarm system for a home or office. A single-wire circuit is laid out around the area that is to be protected. A switch is installed at each door and window. When all the doors and windows are closed, the circuit is closed and the alarm does not sound. If someone opens any window or door connected to the circuit, the whole circuit is opened. This break in the circuit triggers an alarm.

In a **parallel circuit**, each device in the circuit is on a different branch. Each branch works by itself. If one branch is broken or removed, the electrons can still flow through the other branches. They are still part of a complete circuit. The individual letters in a neon sign are usually connected in parallel. If one letter burns out, the others stay lit. Holiday lights and lights in your home and school are connected in parallel.

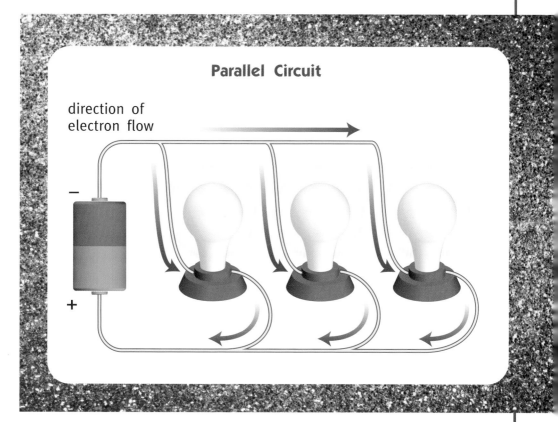

Parallel Circuit

direction of electron flow

−

+

▲ In a parallel circuit, if one branch does not work the electricity will still travel through the other branches.

In this activity, you will make a series circuit and a parallel circuit.

WHAT YOU NEED

- 1 or 2 D-cell flashlight batteries
- 2 small light bulbs
- 2 light bulb sockets (holders)
- 4 6-inch (15-centimeter) pieces of insulated wire, with both ends stripped
- masking tape

WHAT TO DO

1. Screw the two light bulbs into the sockets.
2. Attach the metal part of one wire to the bottom of the battery with tape.
3. Attach the other end of that wire to one of the screws on the first light bulb socket.
4. Attach one end of the second wire to the other screw on the first light bulb socket.
5. Attach the other end of the second wire to one screw on the second light bulb socket.
6. Attach one end of the third wire to the other screw of the second light bulb socket.
7. Tape the other end of the third wire to the top of the battery. The light bulbs should light.

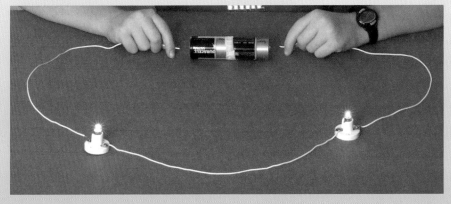

▲ the light bulbs wired in series

8. You have made a series circuit. Unscrew one of the light bulbs in the circuit. What happens to the other light bulb?
9. Take the series circuit apart.
10. Tape one end of one wire to the bottom of the battery.
11. Attach the free end of that wire to the left screw on the first light bulb socket.
12. Attach one end of the second wire to the right screw on the first light bulb socket.
13. Attach the free end of the second wire to the left screw on the second light bulb socket.
14. Attach the third wire to the right screw on the second light bulb socket.
15. Attach the free end of the third wire to the left screw on the first light bulb socket.
16. Attach one end of the fourth wire to the right screw on the first light bulb socket.
17. Tape the free end of the fourth wire to the top of the battery. The light bulbs should light.
18. You have made a parallel circuit. Unscrew one of the light bulbs in the circuit. What happens to the other light bulb?

▲ the light bulbs wired in parallel

Safety

In a house or an apartment, several circuits carry electricity through the various rooms. These circuits connect overhead lights, wall outlets, and major appliances, such as an air conditioner or heater. Almost all of the circuits are parallel circuits that can have several devices attached to them.

Electricity comes into a house or apartment through a heavy wire or cable that can safely carry a heavy load of electricity. The cable leads into a circuit breaker box or fuse box. From this box, the electricity branches out to the many circuits in the house or apartment. Too much current flowing through a circuit can be dangerous. **Fuses** and **circuit breakers** protect circuits. Fuse boxes or breaker boxes are often found in a garage, in a basement, or in a closet.

◀ Electricity comes into the circuits of your home through a circuit breaker box or a fuse box.

Broken wires can cause electrical appliances to short circuit. A short circuit is an accidental connection that allows current to take a shorter and easier path around a circuit. The current in a short circuit moves very quickly and can produce enough heat to start a fire. A short circuit can also cause electricity to travel into a person instead of through the appliance. You should always check the cords on all of your appliances to make sure they are not broken or torn.

Many appliances have a third prong on the plug. This prong connects to a wire in the wall that carries electricity directly into the ground. This can help prevent a dangerous short circuit by carrying electricity safely into the ground instead of into you!

▶
The round prong on this plug is a grounding prong.

◀
If the plastic insulation around a cord is torn or broken, the conducting wire is exposed. This can result in a short circuit.

27

Circuits can also become dangerous if they are overloaded. When too many devices are plugged into an electrical outlet, too much electricity is being pulled from the outlet into the wires. The wires can heat up and catch on fire.

Because short circuits and circuit overloads are dangerous, houses and apartments are equipped with fuses and circuit breakers for protection.

A fuse contains a thin strip of metal through which electric current can flow. If too much current flows through the fuse, the thin metal heats up and melts. The break in the metal opens the circuit and the current stops flowing before it can cause damage. After a fuse burns out, it must be replaced before current can flow through that circuit again.

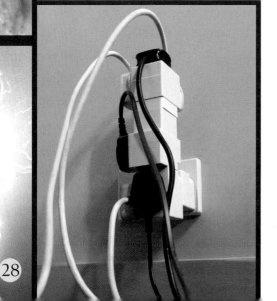

✔ **Point**

THINK IT OVER

Often the term "blow a fuse" is used to describe losing one's temper. Why do you think this is so? Is it an appropriate term?

◄

Plugging too many devices into an outlet can cause the circuit to overload.

A circuit breaker is a switch that opens the circuit if a dangerously high current flows through it. The current causes a piece of metal in the circuit breaker to heat up and bend. This causes the switch to open and the current to stop flowing. A circuit breaker switch can be flipped back into place and used again after the problem has been corrected.

New outlets that are being put into kitchens and bathrooms have small circuit breaker switches built into them. These switches pop open if the current coming into them gets too high. This will protect a person from electric shock. Pushing a small button on the switches can reset the circuit breakers.

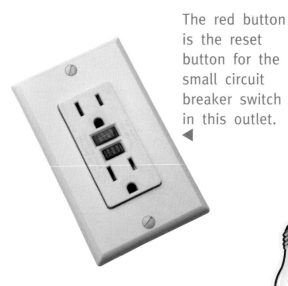

The burned-out fuse, shown on the left, must be replaced for the current to flow again.

The red button is the reset button for the small circuit breaker switch in this outlet.

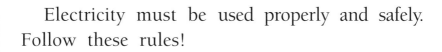

Electricity must be used properly and safely. Follow these rules!

1. Never handle electrical appliances if your hands are wet, or if you are standing in water.

2. Never put anything other than an appliance plug into an electrical outlet.

3. Never touch wires on power poles or wires that have fallen to the ground.

4. Never overload a circuit by connecting too many appliances to it.

5. Never use appliances with broken or torn cords. Never run cords under rugs or carpets. The cords can become broken or torn and cause a short circuit.

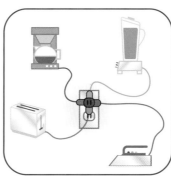

Remember to follow the safety rules when using electrical appliances.

Glossary

atom   **(AH-tuhm) a tiny particle that makes up all things** (page 8)

charge   **(CHAHRJ) a property of protons and electrons** (page 9)

circuit breaker   **(SUR-kut BRAY-kur) a switch that opens a circuit if the current is too high** (page 26)

conductor   **(kuhn-DUHK-ter) material through which electricity travels easily** (page 15)

electric current   **(ih-LEHK-trihk KER-rent) a steady flow of electrons** (page 16)

electron   **(ih-LEHK-trahn) a negatively charged particle that moves around the nucleus of an atom** (page 9)

fuse   **(FYOOS) a device that opens a circuit if it is overloaded** (page 26)

insulator   **(IHN-suh-lay-ter) material that does not allow electricity to easily flow through it** (page 8)

lightning   **(LIGHT-neeng) a powerful discharge of static electricity** (page 12)

neutron   **(NOO-trahn) a neutral particle found in the nucleus of an atom** (page 9)

nucleus   **(NOO-klee-uhs) the center of an atom** (page 8)

parallel circuit   **(PAIR-uh-lehl SER-kut) a circuit in which each object has a separate branch** (page 23)

proton   **(PROH-tahn) a positively charged particle found in the nucleus of an atom** (page 9)

series circuit   **(SEER-eez SER-kut) a circuit in which the objects are connected in a single path** (page 21)

static electricity   **(STAT-ihk ih-LEHK-trihs-ih-tee) a buildup of electrons in an object** (page 8)

Index